POP CULTURE BIOS

JUSTIN
TIMBERLAKE

FROM MOUSEKETEER TO MEGASTAR

Lerner Publications Company
A division of Lerner Publishing Group, Inc.
241 First Avenue North
Minneapolis, MN 55401 USA

For reading levels and more information, look up this title at
www.lernerbooks.com.

Library of Congress Cataloging-in-Publication Data

Schwartz, Heather E.
     Justin Timberlake : from Mouseketeer to megastar / by
Heather E. Schwartz.
          pages   cm. — (Pop culture bios)
     Includes index.
     ISBN 978-1-4677-5715-7 (lib. bdg. : alk. paper)
     ISBN 978-1-4677-6323-3 (eBook)
     1. Timberlake, Justin, 1981– —Juvenile literature. 2. Rock
musicians—United States—Biography—Juvenile literature.
I. Title.
ML3930.T58S39 2015
782.42164092—dc23 [B]   2014021271

Manufactured in the United States of America
1 – PC – 12/31/14

INTRODUCTION

Justin performs a song for adoring fans at the 2013 MTV Video Music Awards.

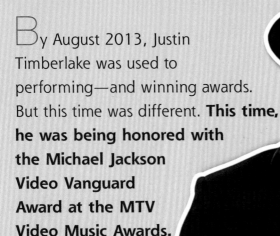

By August 2013, Justin Timberlake was used to performing—and winning awards. But this time was different. **This time, he was being honored with the Michael Jackson Video Vanguard Award at the MTV Video Music Awards.**

After years of hard work in the entertainment business, he'd reached a new level of stardom. He was on the same playing field as other major musicians who'd won the Vanguard before him: Michael Jackson, Madonna, the Beatles, the Red Hot Chili Peppers, the Beastie Boys, and Britney Spears, to name a handful.

Justin holds his Michael Jackson Video Vanguard Award at the 2013 MTV Video Music Awards.

Members of 'N Sync joined Justin (CENTER) onstage during the VMAs.

Justin proved he'd earned the spotlight with a VMA performance that rocked the house. The show opened with a video montage of his solo hits. Then he appeared live onstage, dancing, singing, and shouting out to the crowd.

As he made his way through "Like I Love You," "Cry Me a River," "Señorita," and other favorites, celebrities in the audience went wild. Taylor Swift, Lady Gaga, Rihanna, and Selena Gomez sang along, danced, clapped, and cheered.

Through it all, Justin's energy never quit. And near the end of his show, he gave fans a rare treat. His former 'N Sync bandmates joined him onstage to perform their classic hits "Girlfriend" and "Bye Bye Bye." It was a musical reunion that showed Justin remembered his roots.

While accepting his Vanguard Award, Justin was humble and grateful. He ducked his head and covered his eyes as presenter Jimmy Fallon listed his accomplishments, calling him a legend. When audience members chanted his name, Justin joked that he'd paid them to do it.

"I don't deserve this award. But I'm not gonna give it back," he said with a smile. He went on to thank his video directors, his manager, his family, and 'N Sync—all the people who'd helped him along the way.

Jimmy Fallon presents Justin with the Vanguard Award.

Justin had reached a real high point in his career. But with his enormous talent, he was likely to rise even higher.

Justin as a second grader

CHAPTER ONE

STAR IN TRAINING

Justin as he appeared in his sixth-grade yearbook photo

Before he was famous, Justin Randall Timberlake was just a normal kid growing up near Memphis, Tennessee. Sort of. Sure, he went to school like other kids. But he also spent a lot of his free time singing and performing.

He sang in his church choir, where his father was the choir director. He sang in lessons, with big-time vocal coach Bob Westbrook, who also coached Britney Spears and Lance Bass. Justin even sang in competitions.

By the time he was eight, Justin was polished enough to open a local lip-synching contest. He didn't compete in the contest himself, but he was an extremely cool and confident warm-up act. **He also had the "it" factor that drove girls in the crowd crazy.** After his performance, they rushed him for autographs. It was as if he were already a star.

DID YOU KNOW?

Justin (RIGHT, IN THIRD GRADE) was born on January 31, 1981. His nickname is JT.

MEET THE FAMILY

Justin's family includes his mom, Lynn Harless; his dad, Randall Timberlake; his stepmom, Lisa Timberlake; and his stepdad, Paul Harless. He also has two half brothers, Stephen and Jonathan. His half sister, Laura, died at birth.

Star Search

Only three years later, in 1992, Justin took his singing skills to the national stage. He performed on a TV show called *Star Search*, where wannabe stars in different categories competed against one another to see who could score more points. The performer with the most points got to stay on the show and advance until, finally, a champion was chosen.

Decked out in a cowboy hat and a western-style shirt, eleven-year-old Justin crooned Alan Jackson's "Love's Got a Hold on You."

Justin is all smiles in this fourth-grade yearbook photo.

It was an excellent performance. But it wasn't a winning one. Justin lost to the other singer in his category, a young vocalist named Anna Nardona.

Justin accepted his defeat like a pro. Before exiting the stage, he shook hands with Anna and the show's host, Ed McMahon. He even managed a smile.

But performing was more than a pastime for Justin. He took it seriously. And once he was backstage, the tears started to flow.

SEVEN SECONDS

Making It on *Mickey*

Not long after the *Star Search* disappointment, Justin got another chance to try to make it big. A casting director named Matt Casella was looking for kids to star on a new Disney Channel show. He needed kids with tons of talent. But he didn't want anyone too experienced in show business. It turned out Justin was lucky he'd lost on *Star Search*. He had just enough—but not too much—experience with performing.

This photo of *The All New Mickey Mouse Club* shows (BACK ROW FROM LEFT) T. J. Fantini, Tate Lynche, Nikki Deloach, Christina Aguilera, Justin Timberlake, (FRONT ROW FROM LEFT) Ryan Gosling, and Britney Spears.

Singing "When a Man Loves a Woman," Justin proved he was perfect for the show. In 1993, he joined the cast of *The All New Mickey Mouse Club*.

CAST =
a group of actors who perform together

ALL-STAR

Justin was in good company on *The All New Mickey Mouse Club*. Some of his fellow cast members were Christina Aguilera, Britney Spears, Ryan Gosling, and J. C. Chasez.

Justin (THIRD FROM LEFT) dances on the set of *The All New Mickey Mouse Club* in 1994.

Justin has a big grin for the camera!

CHAPTER TWO

BIG BREAKS

'N Sync members (FROM LEFT) Chris Kirkpatrick, J. C. Chasez, Lance Bass, Joey Fatone, and Justin

As a cast member of the *Mickey Mouse Club*, Justin started a new life in Orlando, Florida. He and the rest of the cast had major talent. But they also had a lot to learn.

The kids on the show took lessons in singing, acting, and dancing. They learned how to read cue cards like professional performers. They even learned how to talk to the media. Since they were getting famous, they had to be ready for interviews.

Fun Times

Justin worked on the show for the next two years. By the second year, cast member Ryan Gosling's mother had taken a job in Canada. She couldn't stay with Ryan in Orlando. Justin's mother agreed to become Ryan's guardian for about six months so that he could stay on the show. Ryan moved in with Justin, and the boys grew super close.

Justin and Ryan bonded by playing pranks and goofing around together. They liked talking to each other in gangster-style speech. Once they even stole a golf cart to drive around the studio.

Building a Band

When *The All New Mickey Mouse Club* ended, Justin didn't miss a beat. By then, he was a showbiz kid. As a pro, he ran with a crowd of talented new friends too.

Ryan Gosling (BACK ROW, LEFT) and Justin (BACK ROW, CENTER) grew close during their time as cast members on *The All New Mickey Mouse Club*.

'N Sync performs to a sold-out crowd at the Mellon Arena in Pittsburgh, Pennsylvania.

In 1995, Justin and a few of those friends formed the band 'N Sync. Members included former Mouseketeer J. C. Chasez as well as Chris Kirkpatrick, Joey Fatone, and Lance Bass.

The band was a huge success. In 1998, they released their first album, *'N Sync*, which sold more than 30 million copies. And things only got better from there.

STAR STUDENT

Justin studied tapes of 'N Sync concerts after each show. He took notes on the band's performance so they could be even better next time.

Fame and Fortune

By 1999, Justin was überfamous. The whole world knew him for his spot in the band. They also followed his romantic relationship with former *Mickey Mouse* cast-member-turned-pop-princess Britney Spears. The couple was all over the media. They encouraged the attention when they wore matching denim outfits to the 2001 American Music Awards.

Justin wasn't just famous. He was wealthy too. He had fun buying Air Jordan tennis shoes and all kinds of cars. His collection grew to include an Audi TT, a Porsche 911, a Dodge Viper, a BMW M Roadster, a Cadillac Escalade, and a Mercedes.

Justin and Britney attended the 2001 American Music Awards together.

SPENDING HABITS

Over time, Justin learned to spend less and save more. In 2011, he told a reporter he bought clothes only about once a year.

It was big news when Justin parted ways with Britney Spears in March 2002. The media reported he cried himself to sleep afterward. His heartbreak showed in the music he wrote soon after the split. But in the years since, Justin has often said that he wishes Britney well.

Musician at Heart

Living large wasn't Justin's end goal, though. His main focus was on making music. For years, that meant shaping the music 'N Sync performed. But after a while, he started to dream of striking out as a solo musician.

"I would wake up every morning feeling more and more of an urge to step out on my own and try my own hand as a musician, just by myself," he said later. It was hard to consider walking away from 'N Sync's success. Still, Justin couldn't change how he felt.

In April 2002, the band took a break after their Celebrity tour. Instead of resting with plans to get back to the band, Justin went to work on songs for his first solo album.

Justin strikes a pose with Cameron Diaz.

CHAPTER THREE

SOARING SOLO

Justin performed some shows with Christina Aguilera, a friend from his *Mickey Mouse Club* days!

As a solo artist, Justin was an instant success. He released his first solo single, "Like I Love You," in September 2002. It soared to No. 11 on *Billboard*'s Hot 100 chart. In November, he released his debut solo album, *Justified*. **According to *Rolling Stone* magazine, the album proved he was more than a teen pop star.** Justin had the talent to succeed in show business as a grown-up performer too. The transition wasn't always easy for kid performers, but Justin had made it.

DEB

first

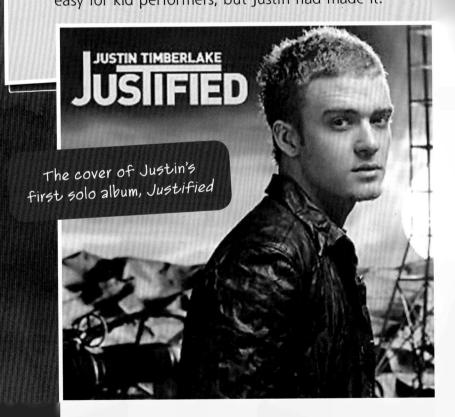

The cover of Justin's first solo album, *Justified*

Justin and Christina Aguilera joked onstage during the 2003 MTV Europe Music Awards.

During the months following *Justified*'s release, Justin worked with well-known professional musicians: the Black Eyed Peas, Nelly, Snoop Dogg, and Charlie Wilson. By June 2003, he was touring with singer Christina Aguilera. He even had a new girlfriend, actress Cameron Diaz.

Justin and Cameron share a laugh during 'N Sync's Challenge for the Children basketball game in 2004.

In this scene from *The Social Network*, Justin talks with Jesse Eisenberg, who plays Facebook founder Mark Zuckerberg.

Movie Star and More

As a musician, Justin was at the top of his game. But he also had acting ambitions. He was inspired by Will Smith, another musician who transitioned to the big screen.

In 2005, Justin appeared in his first feature film, *Edison Force*. The movie also starred Hollywood players Morgan Freeman and Kevin Spacey. Justin went on to star in other big films. In 2010, he was in *The Social Network* with Jesse Eisenberg and Rooney Mara. In 2011, he was in *Bad Teacher* with Cameron Diaz and Jason Segel.

Justin and Jessica Biel attend an event together in New York.

Justin also had interests beyond performing. He launched a clothing line called William Rast with his best friend, Trace Ayala, in 2005. Two years later, he opened Southern Hospitality, a barbecue restaurant in New York City, with Trace and another friend, Eytan Sugarman. His personal life was busy as well. By this time, he and Cameron Diaz had broken up—but Justin wasn't single for long. He began dating actress Jessica Biel. The two had an on-again, off-again relationship, but they seemed to have a close connection in spite of some ups and downs.

HOME COOKING

Southern Hospitality's menu features a Timberlake family recipe. It's for Justin's Grandma Sadie's pecan pie.

Meanwhile, Justin didn't leave music too far behind. He released a second album in 2006. And with frequent appearances on the late-night comedy TV show *Saturday Night Live*, he showed he was even more than an actor, a singer, and a dancer. He had a definite flair for humor too.

In one of Justin's most well-known Saturday Night Live skits, he plays Robin Gibb (LEFT) to Jimmy Fallon's Barry Gibb of the seventies disco band the Bee Gees.

Forward Focus

After his second album, Justin put music on the back burner for a while. He didn't put out another album until 2013. But when he did, *The 20/20 Experience* sold fast—almost one million copies in the first week! Later that year, he released *The 20/20 Experience—2 of 2*. In October 2013, he kicked off the 20/20 Experience World Tour in Montreal, Canada.

Justin performs in New York's Madison Square Garden during his 20/20 Experience World Tour.

SO SWEET!

Justin married Jessica Biel in 2012. The couple had fallen very deeply in love and decided they were meant to be together. Justin wrote a song for Jessica and surprised her by performing it at their wedding.

Justin has a great group of friends to help him deal with the pressures of stardom. In addition to Trace Ayala, his closest buddies include talk show host Jimmy Fallon, actor Andy Samberg, and rapper-songwriter Timbaland.

Justin clowns around with Jimmy Fallon (LEFT).

He planned to visit cities in North America, South America, Europe, and Australia.

Justin has worked hard all his life to become the performer he is today. At this point in his career, he's so huge he can do practically anything he likes. He has no plans to quit—or to even take a break—anytime soon. **And with his amazing talents and remarkable work ethic, there's no limit to how far he will go.**

JUSTIN
PICS!

Justin and Jessica attend the GQ Men of the Year dinner in 2013.

SOURCE NOTES

7   Justin Timberlake, "VMA 2013," *MTV.com*, video posted August 25, 2013, http://www
    .mtv.com/ontv/vma/videos/jimmy-fallon-presents-justin-timberlake-with-the-michael
    -jackson-video-vanguard-award/949141/.

19 Justin Timberlake, on *Oprah Presents Master Class*, OWN, video, 0:52, available at
    Laura Marie Meyers, "Justin Timberlake Reveals Why He Left *NSYNC," *PopSugar.com*,
    May 12, 2014, http://www.popsugar.com/Justin-Timberlake-Why-He-Left-NSYNC-
    Video-34765496.

MORE JUSTIN INFO

Justin's Facebook page
https://www.facebook.com/justintimberlake
Like Justin on Facebook to see what he's been up to.

Justin's Twitter page
https://twitter.com/jtimberlake
Don't miss a word JT has to say! Follow him on Twitter.

Justin Timberlake
http://justintimberlake.com
Get merchandise, tour updates, and more on Justin's official website.

Shaffer, Jody Jensen. *Demi Lovato: Taking Another Chance*. Minneapolis: Lerner Publications, 2014.
Read about another former *Mickey Mouse Club* cast member who made it big.

Tieck, Sarah. *Justin Timberlake: Famous Entertainer*. Minneapolis: Abdo, 2012. Read more about
Justin in this entertaining bio.

INDEX

PHOTO ACKNOWLEDGMENTS

The images in this book are used with the permission of: © Jamie McCarthy/Getty Images for MTV, pp. 2, 5; © Laura Farr/Zuma Press/Newscom, pp. 3 (top), 17, 19; © Kevin Mazur/WireImage/ Getty Images, pp. 3 (bottom), 20 (bottom left and right), 22 (bottom), 26; © Mustapha Houbais/ Anadolu Agency/Getty Images, p. 4 (top right); © Jason Kempin/Getty Images, p. 4 (top right); © Jeff Kravitz/FilmMagic for MTV/Getty Images, pp. 4 (bottom), 7; © Rick Diamond/Getty Images for MTV, p. 6; Seth Poppel Yearbook Library, pp. 8 (all), 9, 10; © Ron Galella Ltd./WireImage/ Getty Images, p. 11; Everett Collection/Rex USA, p. 12; C.W. Disney/Everett/Rex USA, pp. 13, 16; © Fred Duval/FilmMagic/Getty Images, p. 14 (all); AP Photo/Mark J. Terrill, p. 18; © Gareth Davies/Getty Images, p. 20 (top); Handout/Newscom, p. 21; © Mark Mainz/Getty Images, p. 22 (top); © AF Archive/Alamy, pp. 23, 25; © Everett Collection/Shutterstock.com, p. 24; © L. Busaca/ WireImage/Getty Images, p. 27; © Kevin Mazur/WireImage for MTV/Getty Images, p. 28 (left); © Michael Tran/FilmMagic/Getty Images, p. 28 (right); © EXPA/NewSport/Zuma Press/Alamy, p. 29 (top left); © s_buckley/Shutterstock.com, p. 29 (bottom); © Featureflash/Shutterstock.com, p. 29 (top middle); © Kevin Mazur/Getty Images for GQ, p. 29 (right).

Front cover: © Jamie McCarthy/Getty Images for The Tonight Show Starring Jimmy Fallon (large image); © cinemafestival/Shutterstock.com (inset).

Back cover: © Michael Tran/FilmMagic/Getty Images. Main body text set in Shannon Std Book 12/18.
Typeface provided by Monotype Typography.